Jesus & Buddha

THE PARALLEL SAYINGS

Jesus & Buddha

THE PARALLEL SAYINGS

EDITOR
Marcus Borg

INTRODUCTION
Jack Kornfield

CO-EDITOR
Ray Riegert

Ulysses Press

Jesus & Buddha

Edited by Marcus Borg

First published in the United States in 2002 by
Seastone, an imprint of Ulysses Press
This edition published in the United States in 2004 by
Ulysses Press
P.O. Box 3440
Berkeley CA 94703
www.ulyssespress.com

Created and designed by Duncan Baird Publishers
Duncan Baird Publishers Ltd
Sixth Floor
Castle House
75–76 Wells Street
London W1T 3QH

Managing Editor: Christopher Westhorp
Managing Designer: Manisha Patel
Designer: Allan Sommerville
Editor: James Hodgson
Picture Research: Cee Weston-Baker

Library of Congress Control Number: 2004110290

10 9 8 7 6 5 4 3

ISBN-10: 1-56975-461-6
ISBN-13: 978-1-56975-461-0

Typeset in Apollo and Frutiger
Color reproduction by Scanhouse, Malaysia
Printed by Imago, Singapore

Contents

Introduction

By Jack Kornfield

You hold in your hand a remarkable and beautiful book. In our modern times we have had translated for us the teachings of all the world's major religions, the wisdom of the ages. Jesus and Buddha, two of the greatest holy beings ever to walk the earth, inspiration to billions, are now meeting in an encounter of the spirit in the West. When we listen deeply to their words, we find that in many ways, they speak with one heart.

The brotherhood of these sacred physicians, healers of the sorrows of humanity, was portrayed to me in a faraway land long ago. While studying Buddhism I had the privilege of visiting a monastery in the Mekong Delta of Vietnam. It was built on an island by a master of peace known as the Coconut Monk and filled with monks during the war years. Passing along the waterways in the midst of active fighting, our boat arrived at the dock where Buddhist monks greeted and escorted us around. They explained to us the teaching of nonviolence and forgiveness on which they had staked their lives. We ate together.

Then they took us to the end of the island where, on top of a hill, there was an enormous fifty-foot tall statue of a standing Buddha. Next to Buddha stood an equally tall statue of Jesus. They had their arms around each others' shoulders, smiling. While helicopter gunships flew by overhead and the war raged around us, Buddha and Jesus stood there like brothers, expressing compassion and healing for all who would follow their way.

The bond of love depicted by these statues rests on the universal wisdom that they share. They both taught the Laws of the heart, the eternal fragrance of virtue, the path of generosity, the power of faith, contentment and compassion. They both inspired their disciples to turn from the materialism of the world and live a life of the spirit, to come to know the timeless truth, to awaken to the undying. "There is one truth, not many," say the Buddhist texts. It is open to all. "See and know this for yourself," said the Buddha. Jesus pointed in the same openhanded fashion when he said, "The Kingdom of God is within you."

That this is universal wisdom there can be no doubt. When holy men and women—revered elders, Christian monastics and Buddhist masters—have met in recent years, they know one another like family, as living the same life of purity and holy renunciation. The meeting of Thomas Merton and the Dalai Lama was said to be filled with profound connection and delicious laughter. Then there is the story of the old Zen master who met a famous Christian abbot in an airport in the United States. It was a chance encounter and there was no translator present, so they sat together for an hour, holding hands and smiling broadly.

What matters is not the scholarly or theological differences between Buddhism and Christianity, but that both offer us direct teachings, instructions, practices, ways to conduct our lives and free our hearts. Jesus and Buddha say to us, even today, "Follow me." Do we dare?

If we could read, listen to, take to heart and enact even one verse from these teachings, it would have the power to illuminate our hearts, free us from confusion and transform our lives.

Read these passages slowly, savor them. Take them as medicine, as dispellers of doubt, as poetry of the soul, as clarity for the mind, as words that pierce the veil of the heart, that show us the Way, that bring to us sacred blessings.

May it be so.

Editor's Preface

By Marcus Borg

As the world reckons things, I am an "expert" in the study of Jesus. In my understanding and appreciation of the Buddha, however, I am an amateur. I do not know scholarship surrounding the Buddha as I do about Jesus.

As a Christian, I have lived with Jesus all of my life. I have not lived with the Buddha. In adulthood, I have become a non-exclusivist Christian. It seems clear that "the sacred" has been known in all of the major religious traditions, and I do not think that Christianity is the only adequate religion, even though it is my "home."

Thus I write as a Jesus scholar and a devoted but non-exclusivist Christian. Buddhists might see matters differently, and I know that some Christians would. But the cumulative product of my thinking and experience is the conclusion that Jesus and the Buddha are the two most remarkable religious figures who have ever lived.

Moreover, there are striking similarities between them. I have sometimes said that if the Buddha and Jesus were to meet, neither would try to convert the other—not because they would regard such an effort as hopeless, but because they would recognize one another.

The parallels between them are impressive. First, many are found in their ethical teachings, amply illustrated in this volume. The parallels involve both particular teachings (for example, love of enemies) and general principles (the primacy of compassion).

Second, Jesus and the Buddha both had life-transforming experiences at around age thirty. After a six-year religious quest, the Buddha had his enlightenment experience under the Bo tree. Jesus' religious quest led him to the wilderness and his spiritual mentor John the Baptist, culminating in the story of his vision at his baptism. Both Jesus and the Buddha began their public activity shortly thereafter.

Third, both began renewal movements within their inherited religious traditions, Hinduism and Judaism. Neither saw himself as the founder of a new religion.

Fourth, there are parallels in the religious traditions that grew up around them. Both were perceived as more than human, even though their humanity continued to be affirmed. Both were given an exalted—even divine—status.

What happened to Jesus is well known to Western readers of this book. Beginning in the decades after his death and climaxing in the Nicene Creed of the fourth century, the early Christian movement spoke of him as the incarnation of God: the Word and Wisdom of God made flesh, the only Son of God begotten of the Virgin Mary, and ultimately as "very God of very God."

What happened to the Buddha is less well known in the West. Stories of supernatural conception emerged, and even a notion similar to the Christian notion of incarnation. Gautama—the "historical" Buddha—was the manifestation on earth of the heavenly or cosmic Buddha. In some Buddhist literature, he is even called "God of gods."

As individuals, Jesus and the Buddha would not have recognized themselves in this exalted language. Indeed, both rejected even mild forms of it. The Gospels contain a story of Jesus objecting even to being called "good"; a Buddhist story reports that the Buddha similarly rejected grand estimates of him.

Yet I do not find anything wrong with the development of such language in early Buddhism and Christianity. The exaltation of Jesus and the Buddha reflects the enormous impact of these two figures upon their followers, during their lifetimes and afterward.

Though more parallels could be cited, I will mention only one more. For me, it is the most striking one. Jesus and the Buddha were teachers of wisdom. Wisdom is more than ethics, even though it includes ethical teaching. The "more" consists of fundamental ways of seeing and being. Wisdom is not just about moral behavior, but about the "center," the place from which moral perception and moral behavior flow.

Jesus and the Buddha were teachers of a world-subverting wisdom that undermined and challenged conventional ways of seeing and being in their time and in every time. Their subversive wisdom was also an alternative wisdom: they taught a way or path of transformation.

Thus both were teachers of the way less traveled. "Way" or "path" imagery is central to both bodies of teaching. The way of the Buddha is enshrined in the four noble truths of Buddhism, the fourth of which is "the eightfold path." Jesus spoke regularly of "the way." Moreover, according to the book of Acts, the earliest name for the Jesus movement was "the Way." The Gospel of John thus only takes this image one step further in speaking of Jesus as the incarnation of "the way."

What Jesus and the Buddha said about "the way" is remarkably similar. I will mention three major points of contact. First, in both cases, it involves a new way of seeing. Sayings about seeing, sight, and light are central to Jesus' teaching. Moreover, the forms of Jesus' teaching—his aphorisms and parables—most commonly functioned to invite a new way of seeing.

So also for the Buddha. Indeed, the common description of him as "the enlightened one" points to the centrality of a new way of seeing. Enlightenment means seeing differently. Both Jesus and the Buddha sought to bring about in their hearers a radical perceptual shift—a new way of seeing life. The familiar line from a Christian hymn expresses an emphasis common to both: "I once was blind, but now I see."

Second, both paths or ways involve a similar psychological and spiritual process of transformation. The way of the Buddha entails a reorientation of one's life from "grasping" (the cause of suffering) to "letting go" of grasping (the path of liberation from suffering). The Buddha invited his followers to see that life is not about grasping but about letting go, and then to embark on the path of letting go.

Though Jesus did not generate a systematic set of "noble truths" as the Buddha did, the images running through his teaching point to

the same path. Those who empty themselves will be exalted, and those who exalt themselves will be emptied; those who make themselves last will be first, and the first last. To become as a child means to relinquish one's worldly importance. The path of discipleship involves "taking up one's cross," understood as a symbol for the internal process of dying to an old way of being and entering a new way of being.

Such was the experience of Paul, the first Christian writer: "I have been crucified with Christ; it is no longer I who live, but Christ who lives in me." At the earliest stage of the Christianity to which we have access, dying to an old way of being was central to the movement.

Buddhist "letting go" and Christian "dying" are similar processes. Dying is the ultimate letting go—of the world and of one's self. The world as the center of one's identity and security and the self as the center of one's preoccupation pass away. This "letting go" is liberation from an old way of being and resurrection into a new way of being. There is thus a Buddhist "born again" experience as well as a Christian "liberation through enlightenment" experience.

Third, the ethical fruit of this internal transformation is the same for both: becoming a more compassionate being. The Buddha is often called "the compassionate one," and the central characteristic of a *bodhisattva* (roughly, a Buddhist saint) is compassion.

So also for Jesus. When he crystallized with one word the life that would result from following his way, the word was compassion: "Be compassionate, as God is compassionate." Paul's word for compassion is love, and he spoke of love as the primary fruit of the Spirit and the greatest of the spiritual gifts. Indeed, one might even say that becoming a *bodhisattva* is the goal of the fully developed Christian life. As Paul put it, "We are being transformed from one degree of glory to another into the likeness of Christ."

Thus, despite differences in language and imagery, the way taught by the Buddha and the way taught by Jesus strongly resemble one another. In their wisdom teaching, I see no significant difference. But before I turn to some reflections about this remarkable similarity, I want to note one major difference between Jesus and the Buddha.

There is a social and political passion in Jesus which we do not find in the Buddha. In the judgment of many Jesus scholars, in addition to being a wisdom teacher and healer, Jesus was a social prophet. He challenged the domination system of his day and its ruling elites, and affirmed an alternative social vision.

Indeed, Jesus' activity as a social prophet—as a voice of religious social protest—is the most likely reason that his public activity was so brief compared to the Buddha's. It lasted only a year (according to the first three Gospels), or three or four years (according to the Gospel of John), compared to the Buddha's nearly fifty years of teaching. Jesus' early death was probably because of his social-political passion; if he had been simply a wisdom teacher and healer, I doubt that he would have been executed.

This difference between Jesus and the Buddha may reflect their difference in social class. The Buddha was born into a wealthy ruling class, Jesus into an oppressed peasant class. As John Dominic Crossan (in my judgment, the premier Jesus scholar in the world today) remarked in a conversation, a passion for justice comes from the experience of injustice. A second possible factor is that Jesus stood in the tradition of Moses and the classical prophets of ancient Israel, all of them God-intoxicated voices of religious social protest.

To return to the similarity between Jesus and the Buddha, which resides primarily in their wisdom teaching: How does one account for it? The similarity is so strong that some scholars have suggested direct contact or cultural borrowing as the explanation. Because the Buddha lived about five hundred years earlier than Jesus, the direction of borrowing would have been from the Buddha to Jesus.

Scholars have pointed out that Buddhist teachers lived in Alexandria, on the Mediterranean coast of Egypt, by the first century. Some have posited that Jesus might have traveled there, or that Buddhist teachings may have reached the cities of the Jewish homeland, including Sepphoris, a major city in Galilee only four miles from Nazareth.

Popular speculation speaks of Jesus having traveled to India during "the missing years," the decades before he emerged on the stage of history. There, it is suggested, he came in contact with Buddhist teachings.

But both explanations are unlikely and unnecessary. The similarities are not of the kind that suggest cultural borrowing. They are not at the level of specific images or language. They are structural.

William James' medical model of the human condition and the religious solution, described at the beginning of this century in his classic book *The Varieties of Religious Experience*, provides a way of seeing the common underlying structure. Both Jesus and the Buddha offered a similar diagnosis of the typical human condition: blindness, anxiety, grasping, self-preoccupation. In both cases, the prescription for cure is similar: "seeing," "letting go," "dying."

To me, the most satisfactory explanation for this similarity of underlying structure is not cultural borrowing, but commonality of religious experience. Both Jesus and the Buddha had life-transforming experiences of "the sacred." Here we encounter a conundrum of sorts.

Buddhist and Christian scholars in the past have often said that the Buddha rejected the notion of "God," whereas God was of overwhelming importance for Jesus. But more recent scholarship has suggested that what the Buddha rejected was the notion of a personal god—that is, God as a supernatural being separate from the universe.

But there is another notion of God, namely the sacred as "Godhead": as the unborn, uncreated, undifferentiated formless source of all that is, present "right here" as well as "more than right here." In this sense, one may speak of "the sacred" as central to the Buddha.

So also in Jewish and Christian mysticism: mystics in both traditions have frequently rejected the concept of God as a supernatural being, and have spoken of God as, ultimately, "Godhead." To borrow a phrase from Paul Tillich, God (as Godhead) is "the God beyond god," the sacred reality beyond all personalized conceptions of God.

"Godhead" or "the God beyond god" is what I mean by "the sacred." Experiences of the sacred are noetic, to use one of of William James' terms: they involve a knowing, and not just an ecstatic feeling. One sees differently after such an experience, and knows something one didn't know before. What one comes to know is *the way things really are*, in comparison to which our ordinary seeing and knowing seem like blindness.

I think that both Jesus and the Buddha had formative enlightenment experiences of this type. From this new way of seeing flowed their wisdom teaching about the way: a perception of the way we typically live, a perception of the alternative way of being, and the path/process leading from one to the other. The similarities of their wisdom teaching flow out of the similarity of their religious experience, not from cultural borrowing.

The striking similarities between the Buddha and Jesus do not mean that Christianity and Buddhism are identical or nearly so. I accept a common contemporary scholarly definition of religions as "cultural-linguistic traditions." Each religion is not only profoundly shaped by the culture in which it emerges, but also becomes a culture with its own language (including images, myths, stories, and the rituals and practices which embody them). Buddhism and Christianity are thus as different as the cultural-linguistic traditions in which they are embedded.

Yet unlike some advocates of the cultural-linguistic understanding of religion, I see a strong connection between these traditions and religious experience. I see each religion, understood as a cultural-linguistic tradition, as both a response to the experience of the sacred, and as a mediator of such experiences. Thus, different as Buddhism and Christianity are, I see both as having their origin in experiences of the sacred, especially those of the "founders," Jesus and the Buddha. And the similarity of their wisdom teaching points to similarity of experience.

The primary purpose of the parallels collected in this volume is not to make a scholarly case for similarity. We would need to include many more, as well as the debate whether and to what degree the dissimilarities count against similarity. Rather, the purpose of this collection is to provide opportunity for reflection and meditation. Readers will find it useful to ask a number of questions about each parallel. How are they similar? How are they different? And sometimes, by viewing the parallels together, one may have the experience of seeing something new in a familiar saying. The sayings can illuminate each other.

The parallels can have another function, too. As a Christian, there was a time when I thought Christianity was the only way—the only true religion. It was part of the inherited belief of my childhood. There came a time when this belief crumbled, and all religions looked like human inventions. The disappearance of my belief in the uniqueness of Christianity was accompanied by a skepticism about religions in general.

In more recent years, my appreciation of religious pluralism—my acquaintance with a number of the world's religions, and my studies of religious experience across cultures—has reversed that skepticism. The parallels among the religions (especially at the level of experience and teaching about "the way," though not very much at the level of doctrine) suggest that there is something here worth taking seriously.

In short, seeing the parallels between the wisdom teaching of Jesus and the Buddha adds to the credibility of both. Acceptance of religious pluralism need not generate skepticism, but can provide grounds for saying, "Here is something I must not ignore."

And so I invite you to ponder the parallels between these two enlightened teachers of an enlightenment wisdom. The path of which they both speak is a path of liberation from our anxious grasping, resurrection into a new way of being, and transformation into the compassionate life.

Parallel Sayings, Parallel Lives

"Do to others as you would have them do to you."
"Consider others as yourself."

The ideas—spoken by teachers separated by five hundred years, three thousand miles, and two drastically different cultures—are identical.

"Give to anyone who requests it."
"Give when you are asked."

Over and over again in the New Testament and ancient Buddhist scriptures, we discover that the lives, deeds and teachings of Jesus and Buddha are strikingly similar.

The correspondences in their life stories begin even before they are born. In the Gospel of Luke, the Angel Gabriel acts as God's messenger, proclaiming that Mary will bear a child "who will be called the Son of the Most High." Buddha's birth, according to the second-century-B.C. *Digha Nikaya*, is attended by devas who say to Queen Maya, "Rejoice, a mighty son has been born to you."

Here are two cultures as diametrically opposed as the Orient and the Occident, and yet as we delve deeper into the traditional biographies of Jesus and Buddha, the birth parallels, rather than appearing quaintly coincidental, become increasingly specific. Each is born while the mother is on a journey, and neither birth occurs in a house. Heralds are present on both occasions, and they do very similar things, singing praises and announcing that a great event has occurred, identifying the parents and prophesying the child's glorious future.

The correlations among these ancient texts are almost eerie. As will become immediately evident in the collections of parallel sayings that follow, Jesus' and Buddha's later teachings are as alike as their early biographies. Whether speaking of love, material wealth, temptation or salvation, they were two masters with one message.

It shouldn't be surprising, then, that the philosophies they developed drew them into parallel experiences during their adult years. Neither began his spiritual quest until he was about thirty years old, but both soon encountered trouble with the ruling aristocracy. Buddha, a fifth-century-B.C. prince who was heir to a throne in northern India, flouted social convention by consorting with thieves and murderers. Though he was a peasant in first-century Palestine, an obscure province of the Roman Empire, Jesus was fiercely attacked for eating with sinners and whores.

They taught that what is inside a person matters, not his or her outward appearance, and they punctuated their beliefs with actions, revolutionizing the religions of their day. Gautama helped to reform Brahmanical rituals harmful to people and animals; Jesus attacked many temple traditions. Both created religions that minimized class distinctions and eliminated animal sacrifice.

The irony in this seems overwhelming when you realize that the new religions they initiated became the defining points for the greatest cultural schism in world history. "East is East, and West is West," Rudyard Kipling explained, "And never the twain shall meet." Buddha created a religion that had no God. Jesus was the very *son of God*. To Christians, Buddhism was a pagan religion; and for Buddhists, Christianity was a web of false hopes and dangerous myths.

In fact, it wasn't until around Kipling's time that anyone noticed how similar Jesus and Buddha really were. For over eighteen hundred years, from the birth of Christianity until just over a century ago, the mirrorlike nature of their images remained buried in the ancient texts of each religion. Then, in the 1880s, with the escalation of European rule in Asia and growing interest in Buddhism, scholars comparing these holy books began to notice remarkable patterns.

One of the first of these spiritual explorers, a Dutch writer named Ernest de Bunsen, equated the Asian concept of an "angel messiah" with Christ. In his fanciful 1880 book, *The Angel-Messiah of Buddhists, Essenes, and Christians*, he told of exiled Jews from the East re-entering Palestine, carrying in their caravans not only rare spices but a revolutionary idea as well. The angel myth was picked up by the Essenes, a Jewish sect living in the desert during the first century, who applied it to Jesus. But Jesus, de Bunsen claimed, refuted the Essenes and tried to hide the fact that he was the

Messiah. De Bunsen's theory, difficult to believe in any era, was completely discredited with the 1947 discovery of the Dead Sea Scrolls, which are attributed to the Essenes. To date, the remains of about 870 scrolls have been discovered; not one mentions either Jesus or an "angel messiah."

Soon afterward, a German writer named R. Seydel began uncovering strong resemblances between the infancy stories in the Gospels of Matthew and Luke and the Lalitavistara biography of Buddha. But it was a British civil servant assigned to duty in India who fully revealed these parallels. During his off hours, Arthur Lillie developed a fascination with Indian religion and began probing the ancient texts. Around 1909, he published *Buddhism in Christianity* and *India in Primitive Christianity*. Unfortunately, Lillie drew upon Buddhist texts from such divergent places as Sri Lanka and China, and from canonical and apocryphal Gospels alike, failing to take into consideration where or when the texts were written. It was difficult for historians to take the king's civil servant seriously when he cited as evidence for Buddhist influence on Christianity texts written several centuries after Jesus.

An American scholar named Albert J. Edmunds, working around the same time, elevated the study to an objective and professional level. Unlike Lillie and his predecessors, who often placed personal religious beliefs before historical accuracy, Edmunds was rigorous and systematic. His two-volume *Buddhist and Christian Gospels* went through numerous editions over a thirty-year period beginning in 1902. Even today, his writings represent an invaluable source for the parallel texts.

Later scholars further developed Edmunds' ideas that Buddhism might have influenced the Four Gospels; many drew on the Essene connection, which became a key element in most of the theories. Dwight Goddard, author of *Was Jesus Influenced by Buddha?*, actually claimed that Christ followed the Eightfold Path of Buddhism and preached the Four Noble Truths. Another writer suggested that the four Evangelists were introduced to Buddhist ideas which, when writing their Gospels, they later confused with Jesus' words and deeds.

Some mainstream scholars still believe that Eastern thought, particularly Zoroastrian ideas carried from Persia to Palestine by Jews returning after the Babylonian exile, influenced Jewish writing in the centuries before Jesus. But Persia (modern-day Iran) is still a long way from India, and Zoroastrianism bears little resemblance to Buddhism.

Others are more adventurous with their ideas, envisioning Buddhism traveling along the ancient Silk Route as it led through Central Asia to Iraq, Mesopotamia and Syria, arriving eventually in Palestine. They also point to the monsoon winds which by Jesus' day were carrying trading boats from India to Egypt. After all, they argue, didn't Alexander the Great conquer part of India in the fourth century B.C., exposing the Greeks to Eastern ways? And didn't Jesus grow up in a Greek-speaking world just a few miles from a large Hellenistic city? Roy C. Amore discussed this possibility at length in his 1978 book, *Two Masters, One Message*.

Some scholars are still more imaginative, referring to Jesus' adolescence and early manhood as the "lost years" and insisting that the New Testament fails to describe this period because Jesus was traveling in India receiving spiritual instruction from Buddhist monks and yogis. These theories do not stand up to the rigors of historical scrutiny. For example, not one of these researchers bothers to explain why the Jewish historian Josephus and the Roman historians Suetonius and Tacitus, all of whom discuss Jesus, fail in their voluminous writings to once mention Buddhism.

To many people, these questions are irrelevant anyway: It is spiritual truth, not historical fact, that matters. As the most recent writings on the parallels indicate, their value may be more in the eternal lessons they contain than in information about who was traveling the Silk Route. Toward that end, two of the world's most venerated Buddhists recently resurrected the parallels, gazing upon them in a religious light. In 1995, the Buddhist author and monk

Thich Nhat Hanh published *Living Buddha, Living Christ*, in which he acknowledges that "I touch both of them as my spiritual ancestors." The next year, the Dalai Lama himself drew heavily upon equivalent texts in writing *The Good Heart: A Buddhist Perspective on the Teachings of Jesus*. To this great Buddhist leader, the parallels are more vital today then ever before because, as he points out, we live in a world in which cultures are moving ever closer, drawn together not only by economic necessity but by spiritual realization as well.

Both of these men, looking into the many questions surrounding the parallels, hint that the puzzle to which we are seeking an answer is actually a mystery within a mystery. The first is the historical mystery: How could Jesus, living three thousand miles away and five centuries later, espouse the same teachings as Buddha?

If historians have no explanation, we are led to the larger mystery, the eternal one. Were Jesus and Buddha spiritual masters inspired by a single cosmic source, avatars who appeared at different periods in human history bearing the same truth? Perhaps their wisdom was so measureless that each was simultaneously laying the foundation for one of the world's predominant religions *and* communicating the eternal truths upon which both religions are based.

Today, Asian culture overlaps with that of Europe and North America, the world is a pinpoint sphere in space, and continents are drifting together in ways no geologist could ever imagine. Had we read the sacred texts of Buddhism and Christianity a little more closely, we might have realized long ago how similar are both the religions and the cultures. Or maybe we simply should have gone back to Kipling's famous poem and continued reading, continued past the passage in which he proclaims that "East is East, and West is West," past the line where he predicts that the two will never meet, to a stanza that the twentieth century seems to have forgotten, a passage in which the poet ultimately observes that "There is neither East nor West, Border, nor Breed, nor Birth, / When two strong men stand face to face, though they come from the ends of the earth!"

Compassion

Most striking of all the parallels between Jesus and Buddha are those dealing with love. Both teachers invoked the Golden Rule of treating others as you want them to treat you. Many of Jesus' most famous sayings—turning the other cheek, loving your enemies, and the idea that one who lives by the sword will die by it—are mirrored in the words of the Buddha.

"The moral teaching of Buddha," Oxford scholar Burnett Hillman Streeter noted, "has a remarkable resemblance to the Sermon on the Mount." A further similarity lies in the fact that Jesus' words from the Mount represent his most important teachings, just as the Dhammapada, which closely parallels the Sermon, is the central book in Buddhism. It was reputedly compiled in the Pali language from an oral tradition that began with Buddha's initiates just as the Sermon on the Mount and other parts of the four Gospels are attributed to the early followers of Jesus.

JESUS

Do to others as you would have them
do to you.

LUKE 6.31

BUDDHA

Consider others as yourself.

DHAMMAPADA 10.1

JESUS

If anyone strikes you on the cheek, offer the other also.

LUKE 6.29

BUDDHA

If anyone should give you a blow with his hand, with a stick, or with a knife, you should abandon any desires and utter no evil words.

MAJJHIMA NIKAYA 21.6

JESUS

Love your enemies, do good to those who hate you, bless those who curse you, pray for those who abuse you. From anyone who takes away your coat do not withhold even your shirt. Give to everyone who begs from you; and if anyone takes away your goods, do not ask for them again.

LUKE 6.27–30

BUDDHA

Hatreds do not ever cease in this world by hating,

but by love; this is an eternal truth. . . . Overcome

anger by love, overcome evil by good. Overcome

the miser by giving, overcome the liar by truth.

DHAMMAPADA 1.5 & 17.3

JESUS

Put your sword back into its place; for all those
who take the sword will perish by the sword.

MATTHEW 26.52

BUDDHA

Abandoning the taking of life, the ascetic Gautama
dwells refraining from taking life, without stick or sword.

DIGHA NIKAYA 1.1.8

JESUS

Truly I tell you, just as you did not do it to one of the least of these, you did not do it to me.

MATTHEW 25.45

BUDDHA

If you do not tend one another, then who is there to tend you? Whoever would tend me, he should tend the sick.

VINAYA, MAHAVAGGA 8.26.3

JESUS

Grace and truth came through Jesus Christ.

JOHN 1.17

BUDDHA

The body of the Buddha is born of love, patience, gentleness, and truth.

VIMALAKIRTINIRDESHA SUTRA 2

JESUS

I tell you, there is joy in the presence of the angels
of God over one sinner who repents.

LUKE 15.10

BUDDHA

The bodhisattva loves all living beings as if each were
his only child.

VIMALAKIRTINIRDESHA SUTRA 5

JESUS

This is my commandment, that you love one another as I have loved you. No one has greater love than this, to lay down one's life for one's friends.

JOHN 15.12–13

BUDDHA

Just as a mother would protect her only child at the risk of her own life, even so, cultivate a boundless heart towards all beings. Let your thoughts of boundless love pervade the whole world.

SUTTA NIPATA 149–150

JESUS

You know the commandments: "You shall not murder; you shall not commit adultery; you shall not steal; you shall not bear false witness; you shall not defraud; honor your father and mother."

MARK 10.19

BUDDHA

Abstain from killing and from taking what is not given. Abstain from unchastity and from speaking falsely. Do not accept gold and silver.

KHUDDAKAPATHA 2

Wisdom

At the heart of Christianity, which defines much of Western civilization, and Buddhism, a driving force in Eastern culture, lies the same basic wisdom. Both Jesus and Buddha focused on the individual, emphasizing that the inner person is more vital than the outer image, and that each of us needs to look at our own life rather than criticizing others. They use the same imagery of light and darkness, sun and rain, the fruitful and the barren in describing their moral world.

Contemporary scholars searching for the historical Jesus are placing increasing emphasis on his role as a first-century sage. Many of the aphorisms they cite in portraying him as a wisdom sayer embody the same advice that Buddha provided to his followers five hundred years earlier.

JESUS

The kingdom of heaven is like a mustard seed that someone took and sowed in his field; it is the smallest of all the seeds, but when it has grown it is the greatest of shrubs and becomes a tree, so that the birds of the air come and make nests in its branches.

MATTHEW 13.31–32

BUDDHA

Do not underestimate good, thinking it will not affect you. Dripping water can fill a pitcher, drop by drop; one who is wise is filled with good, even if one accumulates it little by little.

DHAMMAPADA 9.7

JESUS

Why do you see the speck in your neighbor's eye, but do not notice the log in your own eye? Or how can you say to your neighbor, "Friend, let me take the speck out of your eye," when you yourself do not see the log in your own eye? You hypocrite, first take the log out of your own eye, and then you will see clearly to take the speck out of your neighbor's eye.

LUKE 6.41–42

BUDDHA

The faults of others are easier to see than one's own; the faults of others are easily seen, for they are sifted like chaff, but one's own faults are hard to see. This is like the cheat who hides his dice and shows the dice of his opponent, calling attention to the other's shortcomings, continually thinking of accusing him.

UDANAVARGA 27.1

JESUS

Your eye is the lamp of your body. If your eye is healthy, your whole body is full of light; but if it is not healthy, your body is full of darkness. Therefore consider whether the light in you is not darkness. If then your whole body is full of light, with no part of it in darkness, it will be as full of light as when a lamp gives you light with its rays.

LUKE 11.34–36

BUDDHA

As a man with eyes who carries a lamp sees all objects, so too with one who has heard the Moral Law. He will become perfectly wise.

UDANAVARGA 22.4

JESUS

Your father in heaven makes his sun rise on the evil
and on the good, and sends rain on the righteous
and on the unrighteous.

MATTHEW 5.45

BUDDHA

That great cloud rains down on all whether their nature
is superior or inferior. The light of the sun and the moon
illuminates the whole world, both him who does well
and him who does ill, both him who stands high and
him who stands low.

SADHARMAPUNDARIKA SUTRA 5

JESUS

Therefore I tell you, do not worry about your life, what you will eat or what you will drink, or about your body, what you will wear. Is not life more than food, and the body more than food, and the body more than clothing? Look at the birds of the air; they neither sow nor reap nor gather into barns, and yet your heavenly Father feeds them. Are you not of more value than they?

MATTHEW 6.25–26

BUDDHA

Those who have no accumulation, who eat with perfect knowledge, whose sphere is emptiness, signlessness, and liberation, are hard to track, like birds in the sky. Those whose compulsions are gone, who are not attached to food, whose sphere is emptiness, signlessness, and liberation, are hard to track, like birds in the sky.

DHAMMAPADA 7.3–4

JESUS

Jesus knew all people and needed no one to
testify about anyone; for he himself knew what
was in everyone.

JOHN 2.24–25

BUDDHA

He was expert in knowing the thoughts and actions
of living beings.

VIMALAKIRTINIRDESHA SUTRA 2

JESUS

The police answered,

"Never has anyone spoken like this!"

JOHN 7.46

BUDDHA

Neither have I seen, nor has anyone heard

of such a sweet-tongued master coming down

from heaven to the midst of the many.

SUTTA NIPATA 955

JESUS

No good tree bears bad fruit, nor again does a
bad tree bear good fruit; for each tree is known
by its own fruit. Figs are not gathered from thorns,
nor are grapes picked from a bramble bush. The
good person out of the good treasure of the heart
produces good, and the evil person out of evil
treasure produces evil; for it is out of the
abundance of the heart that the mouth speaks.

LUKE 6.43–45

BUDDHA

Whatsoever a person commits, whether it be
virtuous or sinful deeds, none of these is of
little import; all bear some kind of fruit.

UDANAVARGA 9.8

JESUS

There is nothing outside a person that by going in can defile, but the things that come out are what defile.

MARK 7.15

BUDDHA

Stealing, deceiving, adultery; this is defilement. Not the eating of meat.

SUTTA NIPATA 242

JESUS

They said to him, "Teacher, this woman was caught in the very act of committing adultery. Now in the law Moses commanded us to stone such women. Now what do you say?" He said to them, "Let anyone among you who is without sin be the first to throw a stone at her."

JOHN 8.4–5 & 7

BUDDHA

Do not look at the faults of others, or what others have done or not done; observe what you yourself have done and have not done.

DHAMMAPADA 4.7

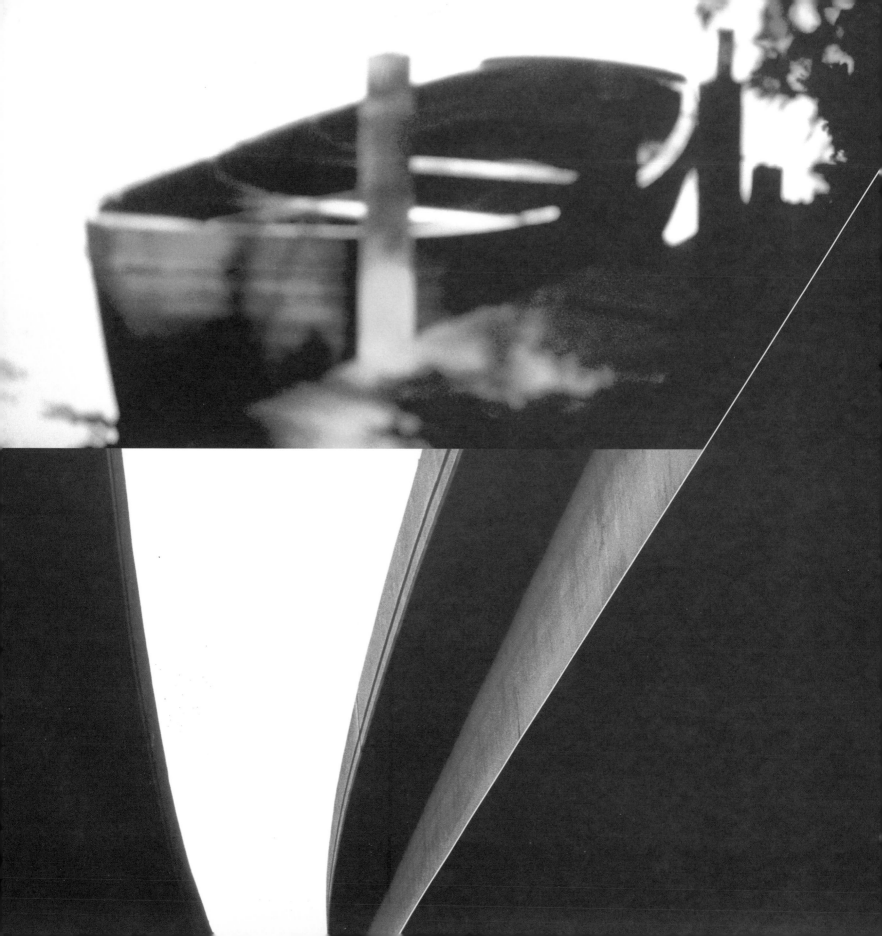

Materialism

Jesus was born to a peasant family in Galilee. Buddha was a prince, the son of a powerful ruler who held sway over northern India. One attracted a ragtag following of fishermen and farmers; the other numbered wealthy Brahmins as well as common folk and outcasts among his entourage.

Proceeding along such different paths, each arrived at the same moral destination. Each realized that wealth not only was *not* the way to heaven and enlightenment, but that worldly riches interfere with our attempt to lead a good life. Buddha spoke in terms of detaching ourselves from personal possessions in order to achieve nirvana. For Jesus, personal enrichment was found in heaven rather than in the marketplaces of the world. He not only would have agreed with Buddha's teachings but would also have marveled at the fact that this rich man of royal ancestry had been able to pass like a camel through the eye of a needle.

JESUS

No slave can serve two masters; for a slave will either hate the one and love the other, or be devoted to the one and despise the other. You cannot serve God and wealth.

LUKE 16.13

BUDDHA

One is the way to gain, the other is the way to nirvana; knowing this fact, students of Buddha should not take pleasure in being honored, but should practice detachment.

DHAMMAPADA 5.16

JESUS

How hard it will be for those who have wealth to enter the kingdom of God! It is easier for a camel to go through the eye of a needle than for someone who is rich to enter the kingdom of God.

MARK 10.23 & 25

BUDDHA

Riches make most people greedy, and so are like caravans lurching down the road to perdition. Any possession that increases the sin of selfishness or does nothing to confirm one's wish to renounce what one has is nothing but a drawback in disguise.

JATAKAMALA 5.5 & 15

JESUS

Blessed are you who are poor, for yours is the

kingdom of God.

LUKE 6.20

BUDDHA

Let us live most happily, possessing nothing; let us

feed on joy, like the radiant gods.

DHAMMAPADA 15.4

JESUS

If you wish to be perfect, go, sell your possessions, and give the money to the poor, and you will have treasure in heaven.

MATTHEW 19.21

BUDDHA

The avaricious do not go to heaven, the foolish do not extol charity. The wise one, however, rejoicing in charity, becomes thereby happy in the beyond.

DHAMMAPADA 13.11

J E S U S

He said to them, "When I sent you out without a purse, bag, or sandals, did you lack anything?" They said, "No, not a thing."

LUKE 22.35

B U D D H A

Then the Lord addressed the monks, saying: "I am freed from all snares. And you, monks, are freed from all snares."

VINAYA, MAHAVAGGA 1.11.1

JESUS

He looked up and saw rich people putting their gifts into the treasury; he also saw a poor widow put in two small copper coins. He said, "Truly I tell you, this poor widow has put in more than all of them; for all of them have contributed out of their abundance, but she out of her poverty has put in all she had to live on."

LUKE 21.1–4

BUDDHA

Giving is the noble expression of the benevolence of the mighty. Even dust, given in childish innocence, is a good gift. No gift that is given in good faith to a worthy recipient can be called small; its effect is so great.

JATAKAMALA 3.23

JESUS

Do not store up for yourselves treasures on earth, where moth and rust consume and where thieves break in and steal; but store up for yourselves treasures in heaven, where neither moth nor rust consumes and where thieves do not break in and steal.

MATTHEW 6.19–20

BUDDHA

Let the wise man do righteousness: A treasure that others can not share, which no thief can steal; a treasure which does not pass away.

KHUDDAKAPATHA 8.9

JESUS

He told them a parable: "The land of a rich man produced abundantly. And he thought to himself, 'What should I do, for I have no place to store my crops?' Then he said, 'I will do this: I will pull down my barns and build larger ones, and there I will store all my grain and my goods. And I will say to my soul, Soul, you have ample goods laid up for many years; relax, eat, drink, be merry.' But God said to him, 'You fool! This very night your life is being demanded of you. And the things you have prepared, whose will they be?' So it is with those who store up treasures for themselves but are not rich towards God."

LUKE 12.13–21

BUDDHA

"These children and riches are mine"; thinking thus the fool is troubled. Since no one even owns himself, what is the sense in "my children and riches"? Verily, it is the law of humanity that though one accumulates hundreds of thousands of worldly goods, one still succumbs to the spell of death. All hoardings will be dispersed, whatever rises will be cast down, all meetings must end in separation, life must finally end in death.

UDANAVARGA 1.20–22

Inner Life

Buddha inhabited an Iron Age world and Jesus lived during the height of the Roman Empire. But both drew their lessons from the basic imagery of the farmland and rural countryside. A good person is like a well-built house. Someone clothing himself in the skin of a gentle animal may be hiding a predatory soul.

It is a simple world, but one pocked with pitfalls. We are surrounded by the misguided and malicious, and in the search for the self there are pathways leading in a confusing welter of directions.

The answer for both masters, the way through this moral maze, lies as much in their imagery as in their message—simplicity. Homelessness is a gift; be like the birds and leave your nest. Don't bother worrying; there is nothing to fear. To save yourself, lose yourself to faith. Don't worry about washing your hands, just keep your soul clean.

JESUS

Beware of false prophets, who come to you in
sheep's clothing but inwardly are ravenous wolves.

MATTHEW 7.15

BUDDHA

What good is hide clothing? While your inward state is
a tangle, you polish your exterior.

DHAMMAPADA 26.12

JESUS

Foxes have holes, and the birds of the air

have nests; but the Son of Man has nowhere

to lay his head.

MATTHEW 8.20

BUDDHA

The thoughtful exert themselves; they do not delight

in an abode. Like swans who have left their lake they

leave their house and home.

DHAMMAPADA 7.2

JESUS

Those who want to save their life will lose it, and those who lose their life for my sake will save it.

MARK 8.35

BUDDHA

With the relinquishing of all thought and egotism, the enlightened one is liberated through not clinging.

MAJJHIMA NIKAYA 72.15

JESUS

Do not let your hearts be troubled, and do not let them be afraid.

JOHN 14.27

BUDDHA

May fear and dread not conquer me.

MAJJHIMA NIKAYA 6.8

JESUS

I will show you what someone is like who comes to me, hears my words, and acts on them. That one is like a man building a house, who dug deeply and laid the foundation on rock; when a flood arose, the river burst against his house but could not shake it, because it had been well built. But the one who hears and does not act is like a man who built a house on the ground without a foundation. When the river burst against it, immediately it fell, and great was the ruin of that house.

LUKE 6.47–49

BUDDHA

As rain leaks into a poorly roofed house, so does
passion invade an uncultivated mind. As no rain leaks
into a well-roofed house, passion does not invade
a cultivated mind.

DHAMMAPADA 1.13–14

JESUS

Whoever blasphemes against the Holy Spirit
can never have forgiveness, but is guilty of
an eternal sin.

MARK 3.29

BUDDHA

Do not let there be a schism in the order, for this is
a serious matter. Whoever splits an order that is united
will be boiled in hell for an aeon.

VINAYA, CULLAVAGGA 7.3.16

JESUS

Out of the heart come evil intentions, murder, adultery, fornication, theft, false witness, slander. These are what defile a person, but to eat with unwashed hands does not defile.

MATTHEW 15.19–20

BUDDHA

One does not become pure by washing, as do the multitude of mortals in this world; he who casts away every sin, great and small, he is a brahmin who has cast off sin.

UDANAVARGA 33.13

JESUS

Whenever you enter a town and they do not
welcome you, go out into its streets and say,
"Even the dust of your town that clings to our
feet, we wipe off in protest against you."

LUKE 10.10–11

BUDDHA

The wise man does not befriend the faithless, the
avaricious and the slanderous, or the one who stirs
up strife; the wise avoid the wicked.

UDANAVARGA 25.1

JESUS

Everyone who commits sin is a slave to sin.

JOHN 8.34

BUDDHA

People compelled by craving crawl like snared rabbits.

DHAMMAPADA 24.9

Temptation

The similarities in the lives of Jesus and Buddha are as compelling as the parallels in their thought. Each is tempted by the devil while fasting during a lengthy retreat near a river. The devil challenges each of them to use his supernatural powers for worldly ends. Each refuses. In one Buddhist text, the devil promises to make Gautama a world ruler just as he does with Jesus in the Gospel of Luke.

The devils, too, are alike. They are lords of death who control an earthly domain and attempt to lure everyone into their web. After defeating the devil, Jesus and Buddha give up their seclusion and defy social convention by teaching among people who have fallen to the devil's wiles. Gautama dines in the house of a courtesan, angering the noblemen of the city, and Jesus is attacked for eating with sinners and whores.

JESUS

The Son of Man came eating and drinking, and
they said, "Look, a glutton and a drunkard, a
friend of tax collectors and sinners!"

MATTHEW 11.19

BUDDHA

They agreed among themselves: "Friends, here comes
the recluse Gautama who lives luxuriously, who gave up
his striving and reverted to luxury."

MAJJHIMA NIKAYA 26.26

JESUS

The devil was a murderer from the beginning and does not stand in the truth, because there is no truth in him. When he lies, he speaks according to his own nature, for he is a liar and the father of lies.

JOHN 8.44

BUDDHA

Mara, the evil one, appeared desiring their ruin, and he closed off the safe and good path that led to their happiness, and he opened up a false path so that they might later come upon disaster and loss.

MAJJHIMA NIKAYA 19.25–26

JESUS

A woman in the city, who was a sinner, having learned that he was eating in the Pharisee's house, brought an alabaster jar of ointment. She stood behind him at his feet, weeping, and began to bathe his feet with her tears and to dry them with her hair. Then she continued kissing his feet and anointing them with the ointment. Now when the Pharisee who had invited him saw it, he said to himself, "If this man were a prophet, he would have known who and what kind of woman this is who is touching him—that she is a sinner."

LUKE 7.37–39

BUDDHA

The courtesan Ambapali, having mounted a
magnificent vehicle, went off to see the Lord. She
approached on foot and having greeted the Lord,
sat down at a respectful distance.

She spoke thus to him: "Will the Lord consent to a
meal with me tomorrow?" The Lord consented by
becoming silent.

VINAYA, MAHAVAGGA 6.30.1–2

JESUS

The devil said to him, "If you are the Son of God, command this stone to become a loaf of bread."

Jesus answered him, "It is written, 'One does not live by bread alone.'"

Then the devil led him up and showed him in an instant all the kingdoms of the world. And the devil said to him, "To you I will give their glory and all this authority; for it has been given over to me, and I give it to anyone I please. If you, then, will worship me, it will all be yours."

Jesus answered him, "It is written, 'Worship the Lord your God, and serve only him.'"

LUKE 4.3–8

BUDDHA

Then Mara the evil one drew near to him, and said: "Let the Exalted One exercise governance, let the Blessed One rule."

"Now what, O evil one, do you have in view, that you speak this way to me?"

"If the Exalted One were to wish the Himalayas, king of the mountains, to be gold, he might determine it to be so, and the mountains would become a mass of gold."

The Exalted One responded: "Were the mountains all of shimmering gold, it would still not be enough for one man's wants. He that has seen suffering—how should that man succumb to desires?"

Then Mara the evil one thought: "The Exalted One knows me! The Blessed One knows me!" And sad and sorrowful he vanished then and there.

SAMYUTTA NIKAYA 4.2.10

JESUS

When the devil had finished every test, he
departed from him until an opportune time.

LUKE 4.13

BUDDHA

During the six years that the Bodhisattva practiced
austerities, the demon followed behind him step by step,
seeking an opportunity to harm him. But he found no
opportunity whatsoever and went away discouraged
and discontent.

LALITAVISTARA SUTRA 18

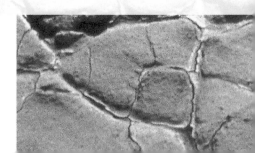

JESUS

He fasted for forty days and forty nights, and afterwards he was famished. Then the devil left him, and suddenly angels came and waited on him.

MATTHEW 4.2 & 11

BUDDHA

I thought: "Suppose I practice entirely cutting off food." Then the deities came to me and said: "Good sir, do not practice entirely cutting off food. If you do so, we shall infuse heavenly food into the pores of your skin and you will live on that."

MAJJHIMA NIKAYA 36.27

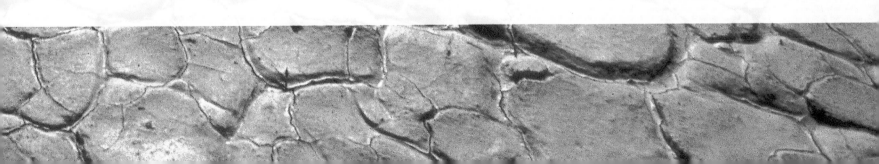

JESUS

One of the criminals who was crucified there kept deriding him and saying, "Are you not the Messiah? Save yourself and us!" But the other rebuked him, saying, "Do you not fear God, since you are under the same sentence of condemnation? And we indeed have been condemned justly, for we are getting what we deserve for our deeds, but this man has done nothing wrong." Then he said, "Jesus, remember me when you come into your kingdom." He replied, "Truly I tell you, today you will be with me in Paradise."

LUKE 23.39–43

BUDDHA

The Buddha performed a feat of such supernormal power
that the bandit addressed him thus: "I will indeed renounce
evil forever." So saying, the bandit took his swords and
weapons and flung them in a gaping pit. Then the bandit
worshipped at his feet and uttered this exclamation, "Who
once did live in negligence and then is negligent no more,
he illuminates the world like the moon freed from a cloud."

MAJJHIMA NIKAYA 86.5–6 & 18

JESUS

As he sat at dinner in the house, many tax collectors and sinners came and were sitting with him and his disciples. When the Pharisees saw this, they said to his disciples, "Why does your teacher eat with tax collectors and sinners?" But when he heard this, he said, "Those who are well have no need of a physician, but those who are sick, for I have come to call not the righteous but sinners."

MATTHEW 9.10–13

BUDDHA

The bodhisattva made his appearance at the fields of sports and in the casinos, but his aim was always to mature those people who were attached to games and gambling. To train living beings, he would appear at crossroads and on street corners. To demonstrate the evils of desire, he even entered the brothels. To establish drunkards in correct mindfulness, he entered all the taverns.

VIMALAKIRTINIRDESHA SUTRA 2

Salvation

For Jesus it is a narrow gate, for Buddha a lofty mountain, but the message is the same. To become pure is the ultimate challenge, and there are few to meet it. Both speak of separating the spiritual from the physical and of following the former while relinquishing the latter.

To do so is simple, but not easy. It is by adhering to truth and overcoming the lure of the world that we can achieve freedom. Be pure in heart, Jesus says; do good and purify the heart, says Buddha. The end that each has in mind is a heaven in which we are free from earthly sin or worldly reincarnation.

Simply follow "the way" I have taught and have faith, both say. And each believes not only that his words point the way to freedom, but that by flouting his message you are condemned to spiritual servitude.

JESUS

You will know the truth, and the truth will

make you free.

JOHN 8.32

BUDDHA

One who acts on truth is happy in this world

and beyond.

DHAMMAPADA 13.2

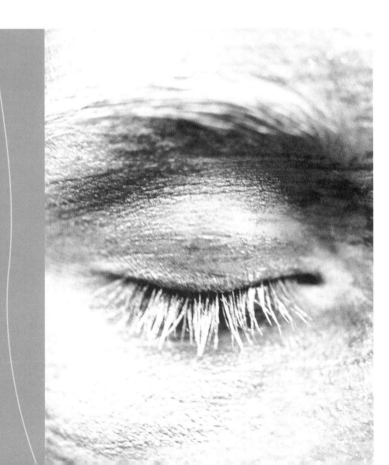

JESUS

Blessed are the pure in heart, for they will see God.

MATTHEW 5.8

BUDDHA

Anyone who withdraws into meditation on compassion can see Brahma with his own eyes, talk to him face to face and consult with him.

DIGHA NIKAYA 19.43

JESUS

Enter through the narrow gate; for the gate is wide and the road is easy that leads to destruction, and there are many who take it. For the gate is narrow and the road is hard that leads to life, and there are few who take it.

MATTHEW 7.13–14

BUDDHA

Just as there are few pleasant parks and lakes, but many dense thickets and inaccessible mountains, so are there few beings who will be reborn among men. More numerous are those who will be reborn in purgatory.

ANGUTTARA NIKAYA 1.19

JESUS

For God so loved the world that he gave his only Son,
so that everyone who believes in him may not perish
but may have eternal life. Indeed, God did not send
the Son into the world to condemn the world, but in
order that the world might be saved through him.

JOHN 3.16–17

BUDDHA

A certain brahmin said to the Lord: "Reverend Gautama,
it is as if a man were to seize someone by the hair who
had stumbled and was falling into a pit, and to set him
on the firm ground—just so, I, who was falling into the
pit, have been saved by you!"

DIGHA NIKAYA 12.78

JESUS

No one can enter the kingdom of God without being born of water and Spirit. What is born of the flesh is flesh, and what is born of the Spirit is spirit. Do not be astonished that I said to you, "You must be born from above."

JOHN 3.5–7

BUDDHA

There are these two gifts, the carnal and the spiritual. Of these two gifts the spiritual is preeminent. He who has made the spiritual offering—such a one, the best of mankind, is honored by all beings as one who has gone beyond.

ITIVUTTAKA 4.1

JESUS

The kingdom of heaven is like treasure hidden
in a field, which someone found and hid; then
in his joy he goes and sells all that he has and
buys that field.

MATTHEW 13.44

BUDDHA

If by giving up limited pleasures one sees far-reaching
happiness, the wise one leaves aside limited pleasures,
looking to far-reaching happiness.

DHAMMAPADA 21.1

JESUS

The kingdom of God is as if someone would scatter seed on the ground, and would sleep and rise night and day, and the seed would sprout and grow, he does not know how. The earth produces of itself, first the stalk, then the head, then the full grain in the head. But when the grain is ripe, at once he goes in with his sickle, because the harvest has come.

MARK 4.26–29

BUDDHA

The yeoman farmer gets his field well ploughed
and harrowed. But that farmer has no magic power
or authority to say: "Let my crops spring up today.
Tomorrow let them ear. On the following day let them
ripen." No! It is just the due season which makes
them do this.

ANGUTTARA NIKAYA 3.91

JESUS

Everyone who lives and believes in me will
never die.

JOHN 11.26

BUDDHA

Those who have sufficient faith in me, sufficient love
for me, are all headed for heaven or beyond.

MAJJHIMA NIKAYA 22.47

JESUS

Those who are ashamed of me and of my words in
this adulterous and sinful generation, of them the
Son of Man will also be ashamed when he comes in
the glory of his Father with the holy angels. . . .
The one who believes and is baptized will be saved;
but the one who does not believe will be condemned.

MARK 8.38 & 16.16

BUDDHA

Just as someone possessed of virtue and wisdom
would here and now enjoy final knowledge, so I say
that someone not possessing that state of mind and
speaking against me will be carried off to hell.

MAJJHIMA NIKAYA 12.21

JESUS

Whoever breaks one of the least of these
commandments, and teaches others to do the same,
will be called least in the kingdom of heaven; but
whoever does them and teaches them will be called
great in the kingdom of heaven.

MATTHEW 5.19

BUDDHA

These worthy beings who were well-conducted in
body and mind, after death have reappeared in a happy
destination, even in the heavenly world. But those worthy
beings who were ill-conducted in body and mind, after
death have reappeared in the realm of ghosts.

MAJJHIMA NIKAYA 130.2

The Future

The great Buddhist scholar Edward Conze once remarked that "When we compare the attributes of the Godhead as they are understood by the more mystical tradition of Christian thought with those of Nirvana, we find no difference at all." Both Jesus and Buddha saw themselves as spiritual guides pointing the way to this "Godhead" and to a future that was free from earthly constraints.

Each one taught that though he would die, his words would remain, helping to guide his followers until the time of what Jesus called "the renewal of all things" and Buddha referred to as "a time when this world contracts." In fact, both of them saw their worldly missions as being incomplete until they had prepared others to recognize and prepare for this future.

JESUS

Many false prophets will arise and lead many
astray. And because of the increase of lawlessness,
the love of many will grow cold.

MATTHEW 24.11–12

BUDDHA

Monks who are untrained will give guidance to others,
and they will not be able to lead them in the way of
higher virtue. And those in turn who have not been
trained will give guidance to others and will not be
able to lead them.

ANGUTTARA NIKAYA 5.79

JESUS

Again the high priest asked him, "Are you the
Messiah, the Son of the Blessed One?" Jesus said,
"I am; and 'you will see the Son of Man seated at
the right hand of the Power,' and 'coming with the
clouds of heaven.' … But the Advocate, the Holy
Spirit, whom the Father will send in my name, will
teach you everything, and remind you of all that I
have said to you."

MARK 14.61–62 & JOHN 14.26

BUDDHA

There will arise in the world a lord, a fully enlightened
buddha endowed with wisdom and conduct, enlightened
and blessed, just as I am now. He will teach the dharma
and proclaim the holy life in its fullness and purity.

DIGHA NIKAYA 26.25

JESUS

I say to you that if you are angry with a brother or sister, you will be liable to judgement; and if you insult a brother or sister, you will be liable to the council; and if you say, "You fool," you will be liable to the hell of fire.

MATTHEW 5.22

BUDDHA

Here, student, some man is of an angry and irritable character; when criticised even a little, he is offended, becomes angry, hostile, and resentful, and displays anger, hate, and bitterness. Because of performing and undertaking such action, after death, he reappears in a state of deprivation, in an unhappy destination, in perdition, even in hell.

MAJJHIMA NIKAYA 135.9

JESUS

Heaven and earth will pass away.

MARK 13.31

BUDDHA

This great earth will be burnt up, will utterly perish
and be no more.

ANGUTTARA NIKAYA 7.62

JESUS

The good news of the kingdom will be proclaimed throughout the world, as a testimony to all the nations; and then the end will come.

MATTHEW 24.14

BUDDHA

I will not experience final nirvana until I have disciples who are knowers of the dharma and who will pass on what they have gained from their Teacher, declare it and teach the dharma of wondrous effect.

DIGHA NIKAYA 16.3.7

JESUS

In a little while the world will no longer be
able to see me, but you will see me; because
I live, you also will live.

JOHN 14.19

BUDDHA

And the Lord said: "It may be that you will think:
'The Teacher's instruction has ceased, now we will
have no teacher!' It should not be seen like this,
for what I have taught and explained to you will,
at my passing, be your teacher."

DIGHA NIKAYA 16.6.1

Miracles

Did Jesus and Buddha really walk on water, pass through walls and raise the dead? Today these miracles, though doubted by skeptics, are as important to some followers as their teachings. The Gospels (particularly that of Mark) and the traditional biographies of Buddha are filled with stories about their power over nature. Christian and Buddhist devotional art all over the world portrays these remarkable feats.

Buddhists hold that miraculous powers result from karmic virtue and the perfecting of the mind, while Christians see them as God's power working through humans. But the miracles themselves are remarkably similar. Jesus worked with loaves and fishes just as Buddha fed five hundred people with a few small cakes. Both were transfigured by dazzling light in front of their followers. And both grew angry when people demanded miracles to bolster their faith.

JESUS

He woke up and rebuked the wind, and said to the sea, "Peace! Be still!" Then the wind ceased, and there was a dead calm.

MARK 4.39

BUDDHA

Now at that time a great rain fell and a great flood resulted. Then the Lord made the water recede all round; and he paced up and down in the middle on dust-covered ground.

VINAYA, MAHAVAGGA 1.20.16

JESUS

When he saw that they were straining at the oars against an adverse wind, he came towards them early in the morning, walking on the sea.

MARK 6.48

BUDDHA

He walks upon the water without parting it, as if on solid ground.

ANGUTTARA NIKAYA 3.60

JESUS

Although the doors were shut, Jesus came and
stood among them.

JOHN 20.26

BUDDHA

He goes unhindered through a wall.

ANGUTTARA NIKAYA 3.60

JESUS

Truly I tell you, if you have faith the size of a
mustard seed, you will say to this mountain,
"Move from here to there," and it will move; and
nothing will be impossible for you.

MATTHEW 17.20

BUDDHA

A monk who is skilled in concentration can cut the
Himalayas in two.

ANGUTTARA NIKAYA 6.24

JESUS

Jesus cured many people of diseases, plagues, and
evil spirits, and had given sight to many who were
blind. And he said to them, "Go and tell John what
you have seen and heard: the blind receive their
sight, the lame walk, the lepers are cleansed, the
deaf hear, the dead are raised, the poor have good
news brought to them."

LUKE 7.21–22

BUDDHA

As soon as the Bodhisattva was born, the sick were
cured; the hungry and thirsty were no longer oppressed
by hunger and thirst. Those maddened by drink lost their
obsession. The mad recovered their senses, the blind
regained their sight, and the deaf once more could hear.
The halt and the lame obtained perfect limbs, the poor
gained riches, and prisoners were delivered of their bonds.

LALITAVISTARA SUTRA 7

JESUS

Great crowds came to him, bringing with them
the lame, the maimed, the blind, the mute, and many
others. They put them at his feet, and he cured them.
Then Jesus called his disciples to him and said, "I have
compassion for the crowd and I do not want to send
them away hungry." Ordering the crowd to sit down
on the ground, he took the seven loaves and the fish;
and after giving thanks he broke them and gave them
to the disciples, and the disciples gave them to the
crowds. Those that had eaten were four thousand
men, besides women and children.

MATTHEW 15.32, 35–36 & 38

BUDDHA

During the times of maladies, true bodhisattvas become
the best holy medicine; they make beings well and happy,
and bring about their liberation. During the times of
famine, they become food and drink. Having first alleviated
thirst and hunger, they teach the dharma to living beings.

VIMALAKIRTINIRDESHA SUTRA 8

JESUS

That evening they brought to him many who were possessed with demons; and he cast out the spirits with a word, and cured all who were sick.

MATTHEW 8.16

BUDDHA

The venerable Kassapa was sick and afflicted, stricken with a sore disease. The Buddha spoke to him and Kassapa was delighted. Then and there he rose up from his sickness and abandoned it.

SAMYUTTA NIKAYA 46.14

JESUS

When he had said this, as they were watching, he was lifted up, and a cloud took him out of their sight.

ACTS 1.9

BUDDHA

The venerable Dabba rose from his seat, saluted the Exalted One with his right side, rose into the air and, sitting cross-legged in the sky, attained the sphere of heat, and rising from it passed finally away.

UDANA 8.9

JESUS

See, I have given you authority to tread on
snakes and scorpions, and over all the power
of the enemy, and nothing will hurt you.

LUKE 10.19

BUDDHA

Now at that time a certain monk, bitten by a snake,
passed away. They told this matter to the lord. He said:
"If this monk had expressed loving kindness to the four
royal snake families, then he, although bitten by a
snake, would not have passed away."

VINAYA, CULLAVAGGA 5.6

JESUS

The Pharisees came and began to argue with him,
asking him for a sign from heaven, to test him.
And he sighed deeply in his spirit and said, "Why
does this generation ask for a sign? Truly I tell you,
no sign will be given to this generation."

MARK 8.11–12

BUDDHA

A wonder of psychic power is not to be exhibited to
everyone. Whoever exhibits these powers openly is
doing wrong.

VINAYA, CULLAVAGGA 5.8.2

Six days later, Jesus took with him Peter and James
and John, and led them up a high mountain apart,
by themselves. And he was transfigured before
them, and his clothes became dazzling white, such
as no one on earth could bleach them.

MARK 9.2–3

BUDDHA

Ananda, having arranged one set of the golden robes
on the body of the Lord, observed that against the Lord's
body it appeared dulled. And he said: "It is wonderful,
Lord, it is marvellous how clear and bright the Lord's skin
appears! It looks even brighter than the golden robes
in which it is clothed."

DIGHA NIKAYA 16.4.37

Discipleship

There is a partial parallel in Buddhism for the biblical stories in which Jesus calls forth his disciples, finding them in Galilee and directing them to follow. But the instructions each gave to his followers are quite similar. Both made harsh demands, Jesus warning that once they had put their hands to the plow there would be no looking back and Gautama devoting an entire sermon to the dangers that could befall an initiate.

Among the obstacles to maintaining faith was that food, clothing and shelter were considered irrelevant. Both teachers instructed their followers to abandon thoughts of personal pleasure and security. As a result, some early believers lost their faith along the way. To those who remained, Jesus and Buddha spoke in parables, a kind of code within the group that others would not easily understand. Ultimately, each organized his disciples and sent them out into the world to carry his message after he was gone.

JESUS

He told them a parable: "Can a blind person guide a blind person? Will not both fall into a pit?"

LUKE 6.39–40

BUDDHA

When these Brahmins teach a path that they do not know or see, saying, "This is the only straight path," this cannot possibly be right. Just as a file of blind men go on, clinging to each other, and the first one sees nothing, the middle one sees nothing, and the last one sees nothing—so it is with the talk of these Brahmins.

DIGHA NIKAYA 13.15

JESUS

To another he said, "Follow me." But he said, "Lord, first let me go and bury my father." But Jesus said to him, "Let the dead bury their own dead; but as for you, go and proclaim the kingdom of God." Another said, "I will follow you, Lord; but first let me say farewell to those at my home." Jesus said to him, "No one who puts his hand to the plow and looks back is fit for the kingdom of God."

LUKE 9.59–62

BUDDHA

He who, having cast off human attachment, has left behind the attraction of the gods, he who is free from all attachment, he, I declare, is a brahmin.

UDANAVARGA 33.52

JESUS

Jesus answered him, "Blessed are you, Simon son of Jonah! For flesh and blood has not revealed this to you, but my Father in heaven. And I tell you, you are Peter, and on this rock I will build my church, and the gates of Hades will not prevail against it. I will give you the keys of the kingdom of heaven, and whatever you bind on earth will be bound in heaven, and whatever you loose on earth will be loosed in heaven."

MATTHEW 16.17–19

BUDDHA

Were it to be said of anyone: "He is the son of the Blessed One, born of his breast, an heir in the dharma, not an heir in material things," it is of my follower Sariputta that this should be said. The matchless wheel of the dharma is kept rolling by Sariputta.

MAJJHIMA NIKAYA 111.22–23

JESUS

He called the twelve and began to send them
out two by two, and gave them authority over
the unclean spirits. So they went out and
proclaimed that all should repent. They cast
out many demons, and anointed with oil
many who were sick and cured them.

MARK 6.7 & 12–13

BUDDHA

Walk, monks, throughout the land for the blessing
of the people, for the happiness of the people, and
out of compassion for the world. Let not two of
you go by one way.

VINAYA, MAHAVAGGA 1.11.1

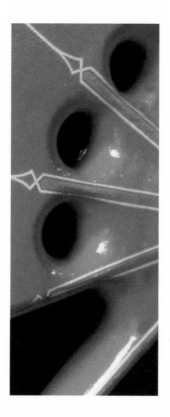

JESUS

"To you has been given the secret of the kingdom of God, but for those outside, everything comes in parables." He did not speak to them except in parables, but he explained everything in private to his disciples.

MARK 4.11 & 34

BUDDHA

Such talk on the dharma is not given to lay people clothed in white. Such talk on the dharma is given to those who have gone forth.

MAJJHIMA NIKAYA 143.15

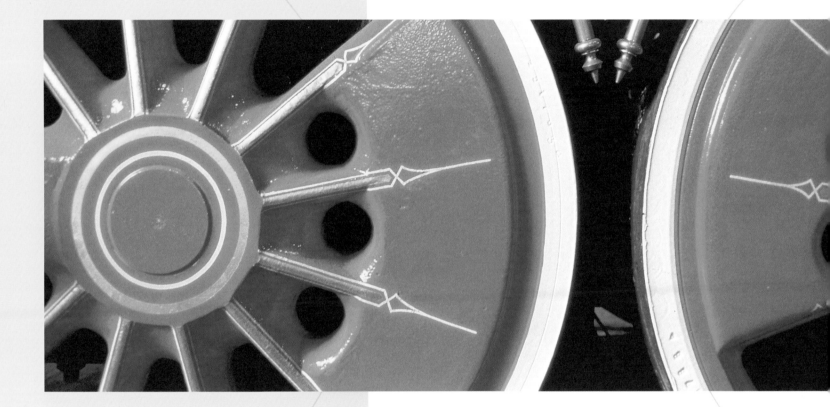

JESUS

Go therefore and make disciples of all
nations, baptizing them in the name of the
Father and of the Son and of the Holy Spirit,
and teaching them to obey everything that
I have commanded you.

MATTHEW 28.19–20

BUDDHA

Teach the dharma which is lovely at the
beginning, lovely in the middle, lovely at the
end. Explain with the spirit and the letter in
the fashion of Brahma. In this way you will
be completely fulfilled and wholly pure.

VINAYA, MAHAVAGGA 1.11.1

JESUS

To all who received him, who believed in his name,

he gave power to become children of God, who

were born, not of blood or of the will of the flesh

or of the will of man, but of God.

JOHN 1.12–13

BUDDHA

You are my own true sons, born of dharma, created by

dharma, my spiritual heirs, not carnal heirs.

ITIVUTTAKA 4.1

JESUS

His disciples said to him, "If such is the case of a man with his wife, it is better not to marry." But he said to them, "Not everyone can accept this teaching, but only those to whom it is given."

MATTHEW 19.10–11

BUDDHA

The wise man should avoid promiscuity as if it were a burning charcoal pit. If he is unable to lead a celibate life fully, let him not transgress with another's wife.

SUTTA NIPATA 396

JESUS

Many of his disciples turned back and
no longer went about with him.

JOHN 6.66

BUDDHA

Sixty more gave up the training and returned
to the lower life, saying: "Hard is the task of
the Exalted One!"

ANGUTTARA NIKAYA 7.68

JESUS

Looking at those who sat around him,
he said, "Here are my mother and my brothers!
Whoever does the will of God is my brother
and sister and mother."

MARK 3.34–35

BUDDHA

Just as the great rivers, on reaching the great
ocean, lose their former names and identities and
are reckoned simply as the great ocean, so do
followers lose their former names and clans and
become sons of the Buddha's clan.

VINAYA, CULLAVAGGA 9.1.4

Attributes

The question whether Jesus was a man or god has been debated for centuries. Both he and Buddha had characteristics of each. Eternal in some respects, both were destined to die. Ironically, they prepared their disciples for this very human event by permitting them to witness a transfiguration in which their bodies became supernaturally radiant.

Various religious texts portray them as remarkable in appearance and liken them to a lion and a king. Most importantly, they are described as avatars who descend from heaven to serve humankind and eventually return whence they came. In both Buddhism and Christianity, they are seen as fully human but capable of miraculous powers. Each is born of a woman—but a chaste woman, who thus combines humanity with divinity.

JESUS

Jesus spoke unto them, saying, "I am the light of the world. Whoever follows me will never walk in darkness but will have the light of life."

JOHN 8.12

BUDDHA

When a Bodhisattva descends from heaven, there appears in this world an immeasurable, splendid light surpassing the glory of the most powerful glow. And whatever dark spaces lie beyond the world's end will be illuminated by this light.

DIGHA NIKAYA 14.1.17

JESUS

"I came from God and now I am here. I did not come on my own, but he sent me. You do not know him. But I know him. I do know him and I keep his word."

JOHN 8.42 & 55

BUDDHA

It might be said that a man, on being asked the way, might be confused or perplexed. But I know Brahma and the world of Brahma, and the way to the world of Brahma, and the path of practice whereby the world of Brahma may be gained.

DIGHA NIKAYA 13.38

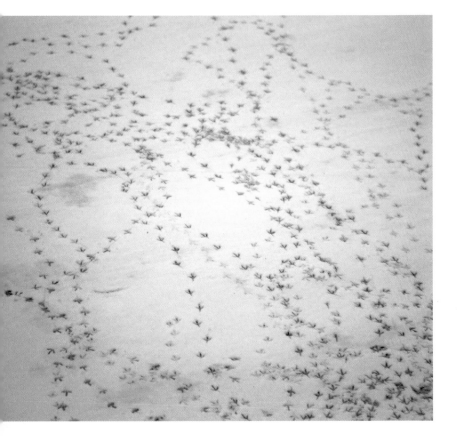

JESUS

Jesus said to him, "I am the way, and the truth, and the life. No one comes to the Father except through me. Have I been with you all this time, Phillip, and you still do not know me? Whoever has seen me has seen the Father. How can you say, 'Show us the Father?' I will not leave you orphaned; I am coming to you. In a little while the world will no longer see me, but you will see me; because I live, you also will live. On that day you will know that I am in my Father, and you in me, and I in you. They who have my commandments and keep them are those who love me; and those who love me will be loved by my Father, and I will love them and reveal myself to them."

JOHN 14.6 & 9 & 18–21

BUDDHA

Even if a monk should seize the hem of my garment and
walk behind me step for step, yet if he is covetous in his
desires, careless and unrestrained, then that monk is far
from me and I am far from him. What is the cause of
that? Monks, that monk does not see dharma. Not
seeing dharma he does not see me. Even though a monk
should dwell far away, yet if he is not covetous in his
desires, not fierce in his longing, not malevolent of heart,
not of mind corrupt, but composed, calm, mindful and
restrained in sense—then indeed that one is near to me
and I am near to him. What is the cause of that? Monks,
that monk sees dharma. Seeing dharma he sees me.

ITIVUTTAKA 3.5.3

JESUS

For the Son of Man came not to be served but to serve, and to give his life a ransom for many.

MARK 10.45

BUDDHA

I am your surety for not returning.

ITIVUTTAKA 1.1.6

JESUS

I saw one like the Son of Man, clothed with a long robe and with a golden sash across his chest. His head and his hair were white as white wool, white as snow; his eyes were like a flame of fire, his feet were like burnished bronze, refined as in a furnace, and his voice was like the sound of many waters. In his right hand he held seven stars, and from his mouth came a sharp, two-edged sword, and his face was like the sun shining with full force.

REVELATION 1.14–16

BUDDHA

This prince is endowed with the marks of a Great Man. On the soles of his feet are wheels with a thousand spokes. His complexion is bright, the color of gold. He has a Brahma-like voice, like that of a bird. His eyes are deep blue. The hair between his eyebrows is white, and soft like cotton-down. His head is like a royal turban.

DIGHA NIKAYA 14.1.32

JESUS

I have given them your word, and the world has hated them because they do not belong to the world, just as I do not belong to the world. I am not asking you to take them out of the world, but I ask you to protect them from the evil one. They do not belong to the world, just as I do not belong to the world.

JOHN 17.14–16

BUDDHA

Just as, brethren, a dark blue lotus or a white lotus, born in the water, comes to full growth in the water, rises to the surface and stands unspotted by the water, even so, brethren, the Buddha, having come to full growth in the world, passing beyond the world, abides unspotted by the world.

SAMYUTTA NIKAYA 22.94

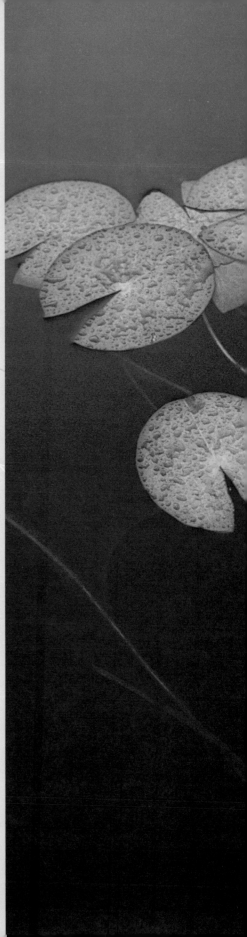

JESUS

The high priest asked him, "Are you the Messiah, the Son of the Blessed One?" Jesus said, "I am; and 'you will see the Son of Man seated at the right hand of the Power' and 'coming with the clouds of heaven.'"

MARK 14.61–62

BUDDHA

This prince is endowed with the marks of a Great Man. To such, only two courses are open. If he goes forth into the world, then he will become a fully enlightened Buddha, one who draws back the veil from the world.

DIGHA NIKAYA 14.1.31

JESUS

The crowd answered him, "We have heard from the law that the Messiah remains forever."

JOHN 12.34

BUDDHA

Whoever has developed the four roads to power could undoubtedly live for a century. The Buddha has developed these powers. He could undoubtedly live for a century.

DIGHA NIKAYA 16.3.3

JESUS

Pilate asked him, "So you say you are a king?"
Jesus answered, "You say that I am a king. For this
I was born, and for this I came into the world, to
testify to the truth. Everyone who belongs to the
truth listens to my voice."

JOHN 18.37

BUDDHA

I am a supreme king. So let your doubts about me cease.

I am the holy one beyond compare. I rejoice free from fear.

MAJJHIMA NIKAYA 92.17 & 19

Life Stories

It is particularly in the accounts of their births that the lives of Jesus and Buddha resemble one another. Both were born of chaste women amid blinding light from the heavens. There is even a Buddhist legend that the newborn child was wrapped in swaddling clothes. Indian sages pay homage to Buddha and the Wise Men herald Jesus' coming. There is also a strong parallel between the ascetic Asita and Simeon, the devout Jew who recognizes Jesus as Christ. Both are old men who inform the parents that their baby is divine and who then lament that they themselves will soon die.

While the birth and adulthood of Jesus and Buddha are documented in detail, there is only a single story about each one's childhood, a tale in which he appears as a spiritual prodigy. Even in death they seem to be fulfilling mirror-image destinies, as the passing of each is marked by terrible thunder and a great earthquake.

JESUS

When his mother Mary had been engaged to
Joseph, but before they lived together, she was
found to be with child from the Holy Spirit. This
took place to fulfill what had been spoken by the
Lord through the prophet: "Look, the virgin
shall conceive and bear a son."

MATTHEW 1.18 & 22–23

BUDDHA

When the Bodhisattva had descended into his
mother's womb, no sensual thought arose in her
concerning men, and she was inaccessible to any
man having a lustful mind.

MAJJHIMA NIKAYA 123.10

JESUS

In the time of King Herod, after Jesus was born in Bethlehem of Judea, wise men from the East came to Jerusalem, asking, "Where is the child who has been born king of the Jews? For we have observed his star at its rising, and have come to pay him homage."

MATTHEW 2.1–2

BUDDHA

For what reasons are these signs revealed? Is it that a god of great merit has been born? Or is it that a buddha has emerged in the world? Never before have we seen such signs! We must trace them together, crossing a myriad of lands, seeking the glow and investigating it together.

SADHARMAPUNDARIKA SUTRA 7

JESUS

In that region there were shepherds living in the fields, keeping watch over their flock by night. Then an angel of the Lord stood before them, and the glory of the Lord shone around them, and they were terrified. But the angel said to them, "Do not be afraid; for see—I am bringing you good news of great joy for all the people."

LUKE 2.8–10

BUDDHA

They took the hermit and showed him the newborn
prince. He was shining, glowing and beautiful. It was like
seeing molten gold in the hands of a master craftsman
as he takes it out of the furnace. To see the prince was
to see brightness—the brightness of the flames of a fire;
the brightness of the constellations crossing the night sky;
the brightness and clarity of the autumn sun shining on
a cloudless day. It was a sight that filled the hermit with
joy, and he experienced great delight. In the sky above,
invisible beings were holding up a vast canopy. From its
center stretched over a thousand spokes. Other gods
waved fans on golden stems.

SUTTA NIPATA 686–688

JESUS

Now there was a man in Jerusalem whose name
was Simeon; this man was righteous and devout,
looking forward to the consolation of Israel, and
the Holy Spirit rested on him. It had been revealed
to him by the Holy Spirit that he would not see
death before he had seen the Lord's Messiah.
Guided by the Spirit, Simeon came into the temple;
and when the parents brought in the child Jesus,
to do for him what was customary under the law,
Simeon took him in his arms and praised God.

LUKE 2.25–28

BUDDHA

The long-haired sage looked at the baby and with great joy he picked him up. Now the Buddha was in the arms of a man who had waited for him, a man who could recognize all the signs on his body—a man who now, filled with delight, raised his voice to say these words: "There is nothing to compare with this: this is the ultimate, this is the perfect man!" Just then the hermit remembered that he was going to die quite soon—and he felt so sad at this that he began to cry.

SUTTA NIPATA 689–691

JESUS

In the morning, while it was still very dark, he got up and went out to a deserted place, and there he prayed.

MARK 1.35

BUDDHA

Then the Lord sat cross-legged in one posture for seven days at the foot of the tree of awakening, experiencing the bliss of freedom.

VINAYA, MAHAVAGGA 1.1.1

JESUS

Fear seized all of them; and they glorified God,
saying, "A great prophet has arisen among us!" and
"God has looked favorably upon his people!" This
word about him spread throughout Judea and all
the surrounding country.
The disciples of John reported all these things to
him. So John summoned two of his disciples and
sent them to the Lord to ask, "Are you the one
who is to come, or are we to wait for another?"

LUKE 7.16–19

BUDDHA

Pokkharasati said to Ambattha: "Gautama is staying
in the dense jungle. And concerning that Blessed Lord
a good report has been spread about: 'This Blessed Lord
is a fully enlightened Buddha.' Now you go to see the
ascetic Gautama and find out whether this report is
correct or not, and whether the Reverend Gautama
is as they say or not."

DIGHA NIKAYA 3.1.4

JESUS

The child grew and became strong, filled with
wisdom; and the favor of God was upon him.

LUKE 2.40

BUDDHA

This prince will come to the fulfillment of perfect
enlightenment. The religious life will be fully expounded.

SUTTA NIPATA 693

JESUS

When they did not find him, they returned
to Jerusalem to search for him. After three days
they found him in the temple, sitting among
the teachers, listening to them and asking them
questions. And all who heard him were amazed
at his understanding and his answers.

LUKE 2.45–47

BUDDHA

Meanwhile, the King, having noticed that the
Bodhisattva was missing, inquired concerning his
absence, asking: "Where has the young prince gone?
I do not see him anywhere." So a great crowd of
people spread out in all directions to look for the prince.
Shortly, one of the King's advisors caught sight of the
Bodhisattva in the shade of the jambu tree, seated
with his legs crossed, deep in meditation.

LALITAVISTARA SUTRA 11

JESUS

Jesus came to Galilee, proclaiming the good news
of God, and saying, "The time is fulfilled, and the
kingdom of God has come near; repent, and believe
the good news."

MARK 1.14–15

BUDDHA

To turn the dharma-wheel I go to the city, beating the
drum of deathlessness in a world that has grown
blind.... Felicitous is the emergence of the enlightened,
felicitous is the teaching of truth.

VINAYA, MAHAVAGGA 1.6.8 & DHAMMAPADA 14.16

JESUS

Then Jesus cried again with a loud voice and breathed his last. At that moment the curtain of the temple was torn in two, from top to bottom. The earth shook, and the rocks were split.

MATTHEW 27.50–51

BUDDHA

At the Blessed Lord's final passing there was a great earthquake, terrible and hair-raising, accompanied by thunder.

DIGHA NIKAYA 16.6.10

Bibliography

Christian Quotes

Holy Bible: New Revised Standard Version with Apocrypha. New York: Oxford University Press, 1989.

Buddhist Quotes

In the citations below, the first page number refers to *Jesus & Buddha*, the next number is the chapter and verse of the scripture cited, and the last page number refers to the edition cited.

Anguttara Nikaya:
Woodward, F.L., trans. *The Book of the Gradual Sayings (Anguttara-Nikaya) or More Numbered Suttas: Volume I (Ones, Twos, Threes)*. Pali Text Society Translation Series, No. 22. London: Published for the Pali Text Society by Luzac & Company Ltd., 1951.
p.84, 1.19, p.33 / p.89, 3.91, p.219 / p.105, 3.60, p.153 / p.106, 3.60, p.153

Hare, E.M., trans. *The Book of the Gradual Sayings (Anguttara-Nikaya) or More Numbered Suttas: Volume III (The Books of the Fives and Sixes)*. Pali Text Society Translation Series, No. 25. London: Published for the Pali Text Society by Luzac & Company Ltd., 1952.
p.96, 5.79, pp.84–85 / p.108, 6.24, p.222

Hare, E.M., trans. *The Book of the Gradual Sayings (Anguttara-Nikaya) or More Numbered Suttas: Volume IV (The Books of the Sevens, Eights and Nines)*. Pali Text Society Translation Series, No. 26. London: Published for the Pali Text Society by Luzac & Company Ltd., 1955.
p.99, 7.62, p.67 / p.128, 7.68, p.90

Dhammapada:
Cleary, Thomas, trans. *Dhammapada: The Sayings of Buddha*. New York: Bantam Books, 1994.
p.18, 10.1, p.46 / p.21, 1.5 & 17.3, pp.8 & 77 / p.30, 9.7, p.44 / p.34, 7.3–4, p.35 / p.41, 4.7, p.21 / p.44, 5.16, p.28 / p.46, 15.4, p.70 / p.47, 13.11, p.61 / p.56, 26.12, p.127 / p.61, 1.13–14, p.10 / p.65, 24.9, p.109 / p.82, 13.2, p.58 / p.87, 21.1, p.95 / p.154, 14.16, p.68

Radakrishnan, S., trans. *The Dhammapada: With Introductory Essays, Pali Text, English Translation and Notes*. London: Oxford University Press, 1966.
p.57, 7.2, p.89

Digha Nikaya:
Walshe, Maurice, trans. *Thus Have I Heard: The Long Discourses of the Buddha*. London: Wisdom Publications, 1987.
p.22, 1.1.8, p.68 / p.83, 19.43, p.307 / p.85, 12.78, p.185 / p.97, 26.25, pp.403–404 / p.100, 16.3.7, pp.246–247 / p.101, 16.6.1, pp.269–270 / p.117, 16.4.37, p.260 / p.120, 13.15, p.189 / p.132, 14.1.17, p.203 / p.133, 13.38, p.193 / p.137, 14.1.32, pp.205–206 / p.139, 14.1.31, p.205 / p.140, 16.3.3, p.246 / p.151, 3.1.4, p.112 / p.155, 16.6.10, p.271

Itivuttaka:
Woodward, F.L., trans. *The Minor Anthologies of the Pali Canon, Part II: Udana: Verses of Uplift, and Itivuttaka: As It Was Said*. London: Geoffrey Cumberlege, Oxford University Press, 1948.
p.86, 4.1, pp.188–189 / p.126, 4.1, p.188 / p.135, 3.5.3, p.181 / p.136, 1.1.6, p.117

Jatakamala:

Peter Khoroche, trans. *Once the Buddha Was a Monkey: Arya Sura's Jatakamala*. Chicago: University of Chicago, 1989.
p.45, 5.5 & 15, pp.26 & 28 / p.49, 3.23, p.21

Khuddakapatha:

Edmunds, Albert J. *Buddhist and Christian Gospels: Now First Compared from the Originals: Being "Gospel Parallels from Pali Texts," Reprinted with Additions*. Edited by Masaharu Anesaki. 4th ed. 2 vols. Philadelphia: Innes and Sons, 1914.
p.50, 8.9, p.222

Nyanamoli, Bhikku, trans. *The Minor Readings (Khuddakapatha)*. Pali Text Society Translation Series, No. 32. London: Published for the Pali Text Society by Luzac & Company Ltd., 1960.
p.27, 2, pp.1–2

Lalitavistara Sutra:

Gwendolyn Bays, trans. *The Lalitavistara Sutra: The Voice of the Buddha: The Beauty of Compassion*. Berkeley: Dharma Publishing, 1983.
p.74, 18, p.399 / p.109, 7, p.133 / p.153, 11, p.203

Majjhima Nikaya:

Nyanamoli, Bhikku and Bhikku Bodhi, trans. *The Middle Length Discourses of the Buddha: A New Translation of the Majjhima Nikaya*. Boston: Wisdom Publications, 1995.
p.19, 21.6, p.218 / p.58, 72.15, p.592 / p.59, 6.8, p.115 / p.68, 26.26, p.264 / p.69, 19.25-26, pp.209–210 / p.75, 36.27, p.339 / p.77, 86.5–6 & 18, pp.711–712 & 715 / p.90, 22.47, p.236 / p.91, 12.21, p.167 / p.93, 130.2, p.1029 / p.98, 135.9, pp.1054–1055 / p.122, 111.22–23, p.902 / p.124, 143.15, p.1112 / p.141, 92.17 & 19, pp.759 & 760 / p.144, 123.10, p.981

Sadharmapundarika Sutra:

Leon Hurvitz, trans. *Scripture of the Lotus Blossom of the Fine Dharma*. New York: Columbia University Press, 1976.
p.33, 5, pp.102–103 & 110 / p.145, 7, p.137

Samyutta Nikaya:

Rhys Davids, Mrs. C.A.F., assisted by Suriyagoda Sumangala Thera, trans. The Book of the Kindred Sayings (Samyutta-Nikaya) or Grouped Suttas: Part I (Kindred Sayings with Verses). Pali Text Society Translation Series, No. 7. London: Published for the Pali Text Society by Luzac & Company Ltd., 1950.
p.73, 4.2.10, p.146

Woodward, F.L., trans. *The Book of the Kindred Sayings (Samyutta-Nikaya) or Grouped Suttas: Part III*. Edited by Mrs. C.A.F. Rhys Davids. Pali Text Society Translation Series, No. 13. London: Published for the Pali Text Society by Luzac & Company Ltd., 1954.
p.138, 22.94, p.118

Woodward, F.L., trans. *The Book of the Kindred Sayings (Samyutta-Nikaya) or Grouped Suttas: Part V. (Maha-Vagga)*. Pali Text Society Translation Series, No. 16. London: Published for the Pali Text Society by Luzac & Company Ltd., 1956.
p.112, 46.14, pp.66–67

Sutta Nipata:

Saddhatissa, H., trans. *The Sutta-Nipata*. London: Curzon Press, 1985.
p.26, 149–150, p.16 / p.37, 955, p.111 / p.39, 242, p.27 / p.127, 396, p.44 / p.147, 686–688, p.80 / p.149, 689–691, p.80 / p.152, 693, p.80

Udana:

Woodward, F.L., trans. *The Minor Anthologies of the Pali Canon, Part II: Udana: Verses of Uplift, and Itivuttaka: As It Was Said*. London: Geoffrey Cumberlege, Oxford University Press, 1948.
p.113, 8.9, p.113

Udanavarga:
Raghavan Iyer, editor. *The Dhammapada with the Udanavarga.*
Santa Barbara, CA: Concord Grove Press, 1986.
p.31, 27.1, p.325 / p.32, 22.4, p.304 / p.38, 9.8, p.263 / p.53, 1.20–22,
pp.235–236 / p.63, 33.13, p.377 / p.64, 25.1, p.315 / p.121, 33.52, p.383

Vimalakirtinirdesha Sutra:
Robert A.F. Thurman, trans. *The Holy Teaching of Vimalakirti: A Mahayana Scripture.* University Park, PA: Pennsylvania State University Press, 1976.
p.24, 2, pp.22–23 / p.25, 5, p.43 / p.36, 2, p.20 / p.79, 2, p.21 / p.110, 8, p.70

Vinaya, Cullavagga:
Horner, I.B., trans. *The Book of the Discipline (Vinaya-Pitaka): Volume V (Cullavagga).* London: Luzac & Company Ltd., 1952.
p.62, 7.3.16, p.278 / p.114, 5.6, p.148 / p.115, 5.8.2, p.152 / p.129, 9.1.4, p.334

Vinaya, Mahavagga:
Horner, I.B., trans. *The Book of the Discipline (Vinaya-Pitaka): Volume IV (Mahavagga).* London: Luzac & Company Ltd., 1951.
p.23, 8.26.3, p.432 / p.48, 1.11.1, p.28 / p.71, 6.30.1–2, pp.315–316 / p.104, 1.20.16, p.42 / p.123, 1.11.1, p.28 / p.125, 1.11.1, p.28 / p.150, 1.1.1, p.1 / p.154, 1.6.8, p.12

Other Sources

Bruns, J. Edgar. *The Christian Buddhism of St. John.* Foreword by Gregory Baum. New York: Paulist Press, 1971.

Bruteau, Beatrice. *What We Can Learn from the East.* New York: Crossroad Publishing, 1995.

Dalai Lama. *The Good Heart: A Buddhist Perspective on the Teachings of Jesus.* Introduction by Laurence Freeman. Translated and Annotated by Geshe Thupten Jinpa. Edited and with a Preface by Robert Kiely. Boston: Wisdom Publications, 1996.

Drummond, Richard Henry. *A Broader Vision: Perspectives on the Buddha and the Christ.* Virginia Beach, Virginia: A.R.E. Press, 1995.

Dunne, Carrin. *Buddha and Jesus: Conversations.* Springfield, Illinois: Templegate, 1975.

Edmunds, Albert J. *Buddhist and Christian Gospels.* 4th ed. 2 vols. Edited by Masharu Anesaki. Philadelphia: Innes & Sons, 1914.

Hanh, Thich Nhat. *Living Buddha, Living Christ.* Introduction by Elaine Pagels. Foreword by Brother David Steindl-Rast. New York: Riverhead Books, 1995.

Lefebure, Leo D. *The Buddha and the Christ: Explorations in Buddhist and Christian Dialogue.* Faith Meets Faith Series. Maryknoll, NY: Orbis Books, 1993.

Leong, Kenneth S. *The Zen Teachings of Jesus.* New York: Crossroad Publishing, 1995.

Streeter, Burnett Hillman. *The Buddha and the Christ: An Exploration of the Meaning of the Universe and of the Purpose of Human Life.* The Bampton Lectures for 1932. London: MacMillan and Co., 1932.

Wakefield, Donam Hahn. *Journey into the Void: Meeting of Buddhist and Christian.* Huntington, Indiana: Our Sunday Visitor, 1971.

Acknowledgments

Contributors

MARCUS BORG, editor of this volume, is "a leading figure among the new generation of Jesus scholars," according to the *New York Times*. In addition to serving as editor of *The Lost Gospel Q: The Original Sayings of Jesus*, he is the author of *Meeting Jesus Again for the First Time*, *Jesus: A New Vision*, *The God We Never Knew* and *Reading the Bible Again for the First Time*. He holds a Ph.D. from Oxford and is a professor of religion at Oregon State University.

JACK KORNFIELD, author of the introduction, was trained as a Buddhist monk and has been a key figure in the introduction of Buddhist practices to the West. He is the author of the best-selling *A Path With Heart* and *Buddha's Little Instruction Book* as well as *Teachings of the Buddha*, *Soul Food* and *After the Ecstasy, the Laundry*. A founder of the Insight Meditation Society and the Spirit Rock Center, he holds a Ph.D. in clinical psychology.

RAY RIEGERT, the co-editor, is a member of the American Academy of Religion and the Society of Biblical Literature. An editor and publisher for twenty years, he is the author of eight books as well as numerous articles for newspapers and magazines throughout the United States. He is the co-author of *Unearthing the Last Words of Jesus* and co-editor of *The Lost Gospel Q: The Original Sayings of Jesus*.

continued

Quotes from the *Lalitavistara Sutra* are from *The Lalitavistara Sutra: The Voice of the Buddha: The Beauty of Compassion*, translated by Gwendolyn Bays. Copyright © 1983 by Dharma Publishing. Reprinted with permission of the publisher.

Quotes from the *Majjhima Nikaya* are copyright © Bhikku Bodhi 1995. Reprinted from *The Middle Length Discourses of the Buddha: A New Translation of the Majjhima Nikaya*. With permission of Wisdom Publications, 361 Newbury Street, Boston, Massachusetts, USA.

Quotes from the *Sadharmapundarika Sutra* are from *Scripture of the Lotus Blossom of the Fine Dharma*, translated by Leon Hurvitz. Copyright © 1976 by Columbia University Press. Reprinted with permission of the publisher.

Quotes from the *Sutta Nipata* are from *The Sutta-Nipata*, translated by H. Saddhatissa. Copyright © 1985 by Curzon Press. Reprinted with permission of the publisher.

Quotes from the *Udanavarga* are from *The Dhammapada with the Udanavarga*, edited by Raghavan Iyer. Copyright © 1986 The Pythagorean Sangha. Reprinted with permission of the publisher.

Quotes from the *Vimalakirtinirdesha Sutra* are from *The Holy Teaching of Vimalakirti: A Mahayana Scripture*, translated by Peter Khoroche. Copyright © 1976 by The Pennsylvania State University. Reprinted with permission of the publisher.

Photographic Credits

The publisher would like to thank the following people, museums and photographic libraries for permission to reproduce their material. Every care has been taken to trace copyright holders. However, if we have omitted anyone we apologize and will, if informed, make corrections in any future edition.

l = left
r = right
t = top
b = bottom

Page 3l Art Archive, London/Dagli Orti; **3r** Spinks & Sons, London; **6** digitialvision/ Robert Harding Picture Library, London (ARC); **12** Photonica, London/Shigeru Tanaka; **16t** Getty, London/Imagebank; **16b** Photonica/Toru Minowa; **20–21** Photonica/David H. Wells; **24** Photonica/Kauro Mikami; **26** Photonica/Image Acquisition; **28l** Getty/Stone; **28r** Photonica/Hiroshi Murakami; **30** ImageState, London; **34–35** Getty/Stone; **38** Photonica/Johner; **40** Photonica/Susanna Blavarg; **41** Photonica/Susanna Blavarg; **42t** Photonica/David Buckland; **42b** Photonica/Nick David; **46** Photonica/Olof Heditjarn; **48** Photonica/Dan Holmberg; **51** Photonica/James Bartholomew; **53** Bruce Coleman/ Natural Selection Inc.; **54t** Photonica/Colin Samuels; **54b** ImageState; **57** Getty/Stone; **60–61** Photonica/Starrex; **64–65** Photonica/Ryuic Hisato; **66t** Photonica/Johner; **66b** Getty/Telegraph; **69** Photonica/Alex Maclean; **72–73** Photonica/Jake Wyman; **74–75** ImageState; **77** Bruce Coleman/John G. Fuller; **80l** Getty/Imagebank; **80r** Photonica/B Schmid; **83** Photonica/Johner; **84–85** Photonica/William Huber; **88–89** Getty/Imagebank; **92–93** Photonica/Johner; **94t** Photonica/Steven Weinberg; **94b** Photonica/Johner; **96** Photonica/Takashi Mizushumi; **98–99** Photonica/Sharon Smith; **102t** Getty/Imagebank; **102b** Getty/Imagebank; **104–105** Photonica/Jake Rejs; **107** Photonica/Michael Gersinger; **111** Photonica/Stephan Kinnmark; **112–113** Photonica/ Jun Kishimoto; **116** Photonica/Colin Samuels; **118l** Photonica/Charles Gullung; **118r** Getty/Stone; **120–121** Getty/Imagebank; **125** ImageState; **129** Photonica/Jake Rejs; **130t** Bruce Coleman; **130b** Photonica/James Dunn; **132–133** Photonica/Michaiharu Okubo; **134** Photonica/Chris Weil ; **138–139** Getty/Stone; **142t** Photonica/Johner; **142b** Getty/Stone; **145** Photonica/Yutaka Ijima; **146** Photonica/Yukimasa Hirota; **150** Bruce Coleman/Natural Selection Inc; **154–155** Getty/Stone